PROTECTING YOUR IDENTITY

A JOB SEEKER'S GUIDE TO ONLINE PRIVACY

AF528363

PROTECTING YOUR IDENTITY

A JOB SEEKER'S GUIDE TO ONLINE PRIVACY

Sachin Diwakar

Co-Author Neha Boricha

Worldwide Published by

Pendown Press

PENDOWN PRESS LLP

An ISO 9001 & ISO 14001 Certified Co.,

Regd. Office: 3767A, Kanhaiya Nagar,

Tri Nagar, Delhi-110035

Ph.: 8130886000, 9650072927

E-mail: info@pendownpress.com

Branch Office: 1A/2A, 20, Hari Sadan, Ansari Road,

Daryaganj, New Delhi-110002

Ph.: 011-45794768

Website: PendownPress.com

Edition: 2024

Price: ₹ 299/-

ISBN: 978-93-6338-955-7

All Rights Reserved

All the ideas and thoughts in this book are given by the author and he is responsible for the treatise, facts and dialogues used in this book. He is also responsible for the used pictures and the permission to use them in this book. Copyright of this book is reserved with the author. The publisher does not have any responsibility for the above-mentioned matters. No part of this publication may be reproduced, distributed, or transmitted in any form or by any means, including photocopying, recording, or other electronic or mechanical methods, without the prior written permission of the publisher and author.

Layout and Cover Designed by Pendown Graphics Team

Printed and Bound in India by Thomson Press India Ltd.

To all the job seekers out there—may you find not only the career of your dreams, but also the peace of mind that comes from knowing your journey is safe and secure.

TABLE OF CONTENTS

Preface

In today's digital world, the job search process has evolved significantly. With a few clicks, you can apply for jobs across the globe, connect with employers, and showcase your skills to a broad audience. While this transformation has opened countless opportunities, it has also introduced serious risks to job seekers—particularly when it comes to online privacy and the protection of personal information.

As the founder of **MySafeResume.com** and the author of this book, Sachin Diwakar, along with co-author Neha Boricha, has experienced firsthand the challenges of navigating a digital job market while keeping sensitive information safe. Protecting Your Identity: A Job Seeker's Guide to Online Privacy was born out of their passion to help others safeguard their data and ensure that job seekers can pursue new career opportunities without fear of identity theft, scams, or privacy breaches.

The internet has become a double-edged sword. On the one hand, it has made information more accessible, connections easier to build, and jobs more readily available. On the other hand, it has also made it simpler for cybercriminals to exploit personal data. This book serves as a comprehensive guide to help you stay one step ahead. Whether you're applying for your first job or are a seasoned professional, the principles in this book are relevant, actionable, and designed to give you control over your online presence.

Throughout the chapters, we will walk you through various tools, strategies, and best practices to protect your identity during the job search process. From setting up secure resumes and protecting sensitive information to recognizing red flags in job offers, this book provides you with a clear roadmap to a safer job search experience.

Our mission is simple: to equip you with the knowledge and resources needed to protect your personal information while searching for new career opportunities. We believe that securing your data is just as important as securing the right job.

We hope that this book not only informs you but also empowers you. Thank you for trusting us to guide you through this crucial aspect of your job search journey. Your privacy and security are worth defending—and we're here to help you do just that.

Sachin Diwakar ***(Author & Founder of MySafeResume.com)***

Neha Boricha ***(Co-Author)***

Acknowledgements

I would like to extend my deepest gratitude to all those who have supported me throughout the creation of this book. To my family, your unwavering support and understanding have been my foundation. Your patience and love have enabled me to dedicate countless hours to this endeavour. I am forever grateful for your encouragement and belief in me.

A special thanks to my incredible team. Your dedication, hard work, and collaborative spirit have been vital in bringing this book to fruition. Each of you has played a crucial role in this journey, and I am thankful for your contributions.

Lastly, I would like to extend a heartfelt thank you to my friend, Dinesh Verma, CEO of Pendown Press, and his dedicated team. Your unwavering support, insightful suggestions, and encouragement throughout the creative process have been invaluable.

With heartfelt thanks,

Sachin Diwakar

Acknowledgements

I am deeply thankful to everyone who has supported me throughout the writing of this book. To Mr. Sachin Diwakar, your guidance and encouragement have been a source of great inspiration. Your expertise has helped me navigate how the digital world works, allowing me to contribute meaningfully to this book.

To my family, thank you for your unwavering support and understanding. Your love and patience have given me the strength to balance my professional and personal life while working on this project. I am eternally grateful for your belief in my vision.

I also want to express my sincere appreciation to our fantastic team. Your hard work, creativity, and dedication have been instrumental in bringing this book to life. I am grateful for your commitment and teamwork throughout this journey.

With sincere thanks,

Neha Boricha

Author's Corner

*****

"I understand the challenges and vulnerabilities that job seekers face today. In the age of AI, safeguarding your identity and other personal details has become a must-do thing. My own experience with online scammers was a stark reminder of how crucial it is to protect our personal information in the digital age. I wrote this book to share my insights and to provide you with the right knowledge to safeguard your identity as you embark on your job search. It is my hope that through the lessons and strategies outlined in this book, you will feel more secure and confident in your pursuit of career opportunities. Remember, your personal information is valuable, and protecting it is essential. Stay vigilant, stay informed, and take control of your online presence."

Sachin Diwakar

Founder of MySafeResume.com and Author of Protecting Your Identity: A Job Seeker's Guide to Online Privacy

PROTECTING YOUR IDENTITY
A Job Seeker's Guide to Online Privacy

"I'm passionate about helping individuals navigate their career paths without falling prey to online frauds or experiencing undue stress during their job search. So I hope this book empowers you to take proactive steps in protecting yourself online, ensuring that your job search is a positive and secure experience. Thank you for allowing us to be part of your journey."

Co-author, Neha Boricha

Chapter 1

Introduction: Navigating The Digital Job Search Safely

It is everyone's ambition to achieve their goals, especially their dream job! Working in a field that has always been your passion feels so great. When you're passionate about what you do, a job doesn't feel like work at all.

Sometimes, hunting for your dream job in any desired field can become time-consuming and even depressing. You send your resume to hundreds of companies daily through numerous portals, apps, emails, WhatsApp, etc. But despite all that effort, you keep a close eye on just one thing—your email inbox, waiting for a response.

But wait, did you sense something wrong here? We bet you didn't! Before sharing your resume, did you thoroughly cross-check the company profiles, their websites, and the details of the employer or recruiter?

Now you must be wondering, "What's there to check? Every company seems legit, and they post jobs on well-known authentic website or apps." Well, did you know that there are thousands of fraudsters posting fake job vacancies on the internet, including popular job search sites? Are you aware that these scammers can access your personal data from your resume within seconds?

We're not here to scare you, but this is the reality of our ever-growing digital world! We agree that various online platforms regularly provide better job opportunities. However, just a single encounter with a scammer can change your life upside down. You never know—your information might be visible or sold to third parties for various reasons; only a few reasons might be right.

The reality is, many job seekers are falling prey to such scams. As humans, when we don't know the complete story, we assume it is not harmful. And in our rush to find a job, we tend to ignore little things. But do you know what's even scarier about your job hunting journey? The information in your resume can be copied and used to create fake documents. Yes, you read this right!

Unfortunately, there are various job scams out there that many job seekers are unaware of. So that is why we are writing this book! This read will serve as an eye-opener to you and others. Besides, it will help you learn about various scams and how to keep yourself safe while looking for a job on digital platforms.

On the other hand, some job seekers are aware of these scams and have genuine concerns about their data security and online privacy. In fact, we did a small survey on such job seekers' concerns that could help us understand more in detail. The final data shocked us to the core, which revealed most job seekers are worried about the personal data in their resumes being misused by fraudsters. And after the invention of AI, these scammers are coming up with new tricks to lure job seekers and gain access to their data.

Every person faces different issues in their job search, so we scoured the internet and found eight types of job seekers who are at high risk of losing their online privacy. Once you understand this, you will realize how vulnerable each job candidate is at every level.

Eight Types of Job Seekers and Their Vulnerabilities

Type 1: Recent Graduates (High Vulnerability)

Once a student graduates from college, they start looking for a job. These job seekers are highly vulnerable because they might have limited knowledge about online scams and how to keep their data safe on the internet.

We understand that these individuals are eager to get into the mainstream by all means. This eagerness makes them prone to scams, like quick employment offers that require payment or fees, sharing personal details, or sharing sample work.

What Makes Them Vulnerable?
As a fresher in the job market, they have no experience in identifying fraudulent job offers.
Seeing their peer groups settling down in their lives, a graduate feels highly motivated to secure any job without checking the details about the job postings.
They are among the most vulnerable job-seeker groups without prior knowledge of online security and privacy settings.

Type 2: Mid-Career Professionals (Medium Vulnerability)

Next comes the mid-career professionals, who fall into the medium vulnerable category. They might have good work experience and possess enough knowledge about the latest online security to keep themselves safe. Even if job seekers in this category are generally more alert than graduates, they can still encounter scammers.

What Makes Them Vulnerable?
Applying for various job postings and having conversations with different recruiters on multiple platforms makes them vulnerable to scams.
Following a carefree approach, assuming they know enough about online safety and are completely safe.
Trying to juggle between their current job while seeking a new job makes them assume they are saving time. However, they are making things easier for cybercriminals by sharing their CVs everywhere.

Type 3: Career Changers (High Vulnerability)

Some job seekers hop from one job to another in search of better opportunities and higher pay. They are just as vulnerable as graduates because they venture into unfamiliar industries for work. Furthermore, they are always on the job hunt and looking for new work, which can make them encounter job scammers.

What Makes Them Vulnerable?
They have limited knowledge about the new job profile, the industry, and the norms and risks associated with job searching.
They often avoid security checks while switching from an old job to a new one and get scammed.
Trying to juggle between their current job while seeking a new job makes them assume they are saving time. However, they are making things easier for cybercriminals by sharing their CVs everywhere.

Type 4: Executive-Level Professionals (Medium Vulnerability)

Then comes the executive-level professionals secretly hunting for jobs under their boss's nose. Although they have the right tools, networks, and resources for the new job search, they might still become victims of cybercrime because of their high-profile status.

What Makes Them Vulnerable?
Executive-level professionals always look for fresh opportunities discreetly by avoiding public job boards. Thus, they might venture into unknown sites, which makes them prey to cybercriminals.
They are on every cybercriminal's radar because of their high status. Their data holds a lot of value, which might benefit the scammers.
Such job seekers end up risking their colleagues' identities. This happens when the cybercriminals try phishing, leading to security concerns.

Type 5: Freelancers and Gig Workers (Medium Vulnerability)

Job seekers in this category search for jobs on every work platform, including unknown websites. They are constantly trying to find new gigs, which can make them targets for identity theft, job payment scams, and more.

What Makes Them Vulnerable?
Regular job hunts can make them an easy target for job scams.
They are active on many job sites and often forget to switch on the privacy settings.
They want to find jobs quickly, which may lead to less careful vetting of work opportunities.

Type 6: Returning to the Workforce (High Vulnerability)

Some job seekers take a break from work for a year or two due to personal reasons. When they try to restart their careers, they are also prone to scams because of limited knowledge about safe job-hunting practices.

What Makes Them Vulnerable?
Since these job searchers are less knowledgeable about new job apps and websites, they may forget to turn on the privacy settings that safeguard their personal information.
They are highly motivated and optimistic about their new job roles, so they mostly avoid red flags, such as cross-checking company information.
Such job hunters are unaware of current cyber threats and what measures to follow to protect their privacy.

Type 7: International Job Seekers (High Vulnerability)

Next on the list are international job seekers looking for jobs in a foreign land. While they are busy solving work permit and visa issues, they are likely caught up in international job scams and identity thefts.

What Makes Them Vulnerable?
They are unfamiliar with the job market and employment laws of a foreign country.
When living in a new country, they may have limited financial resources, which can lead them to accept any job or high-paying role.
While applying for work permits and visas, they are often required to share personal data.

Type 8: Veterans and Military Personnel (Low Vulnerability)

Military personnel and veterans know a lot about online safety. However, these types of job seekers may fall into cyber traps.

What Makes Them Vulnerable?
They may lack knowledge about current civilian job practices and technologies because they have lived half of their lives in cyber-protected zones.
After providing their personal information, they can fall prey to identity theft after applying for civilian jobs.
They may be on a cybercriminal's radar because they have veteran benefits or retirement advantages.

By now, you must have understood that job scams are not just limited to paying fees for jobs; they are much more than that and terrifying. But with our proper guidance, you can protect your identity online. In the next chapter, we will discuss the potential risks in more detail.

Chapter-2

Understanding The Risks

The Dark Side of Online Job Hunting

Your personal data is a valuable asset — your unique identity. Additional information like contact details, address, education, and work history makes you stand out. But what if it gets stolen for the wrong reasons?

Whenever you post your resume online, there is a high chance that your sensitive information will be used for malicious purposes. Moreover, you don't know who is accessing your data and how often it is shared online, right?

As we said above, your personal information is your unique identity. However, it can also be a treasure waiting to be uncovered by cyber criminals. That is why you must be aware of the risks and frauds that can occur online after sharing or uploading your resume. Let's learn about different scams and frauds and understand how they work.

Types of Fraud and Scams

1. dentity Theft

Identity theft happens when someone steals your personal data, such as name, address, date of birth, financial details, and social security number. The victim may not be aware of it until significant damage has already been done. In simple terms, the sole purpose of the scammer is to gain money by using your identity & other details.

Know How It Happens:

- Cybercriminals can access your resume and easily download and extract your sensitive information.
- Your details are stored and may be sold or used to file tax returns, apply for loans, or open new credit accounts in your name.
- This can severely damage your credit score, leading to significant financial loss.

Real-Life Example

Jane, a recent graduate, posted her resume on multiple job boards. A few weeks later, she noticed unfamiliar transactions in her bank account. After an investigation, she discovered that her identity had been stolen and fraudulent credit cards had been issued in her name. Jane spent months working with financial institutions to resolve the issue and restore her credit.

2. Financial Fraud

A financial fraud involves cybercriminals accessing your bank details and making illegal transactions to drain your bank accounts. Thus, the victim suffers a heavy financial loss and might end up losing all of their life savings.

Know How It Happens:

- Firstly, cybercriminals may act as potential employers and offer you a job instantly.
- Next, they may ask for your bank details by pretending to make a payment.
- They may use your data to perform fraudulent activities, such as draining your bank accounts and making unauthorized transactions.

Real-Life Example

John received a job offer via email that seemed legitimate. The "employer" asked for his bank details to set up a direct deposit. Soon after providing this information, John noticed large sums of money missing from his account. The job offer was fake, and John became a victim of financial fraud.

3. Employment Scams

Well, this is one of the most common scams these days! The fraud parties pose as reputed companies and offer good-to-be-true jobs with excellent packages. Their sole purpose is to steal your money or information.

Know How It Happens:

- The scammer creates a fake job listing on professional job websites or apps. Otherwise, they might extract your email IDs and send you the best job offers by pretending to be a legitimate company or employer. Their professionalism can fool anyone because they are professional scammers.
- Next, they ask the job seekers to pay a certain amount as a part of stationery or application fees.
- Later, they also request other details, such as address, bank information, and date of birth, to do a background check or send payment.

Real-Life Example

Lisa, a career changer, was eager to find a new opportunity. She applied to a job posting that required an upfront fee for a background check. After paying the fee and providing her personal details, she did not hear back from the company. She later realized it was a scam to steal her money and information.

4. Phishing

Do not mistake "phishing" for "fishing" because both meanings differ. Jokes apart, phishing means attempting to access your data by acting as a reputed and trustworthy source. The scammers attach company logos, official websites, and other fake details related to the job, which can seem very professional. And trust us, nobody wants to get caught up in job phishing scams!

Know How It Happens:

- Cybercriminals send formal emails or personalized messages on WhatsApp that seem trustworthy and convincing.
- They ask you to open a hideous link and fill in the required details.
- Once you are convinced and enter all your private data, the hacker on the other end steals your information and exhausts your bank accounts within minutes.
- Ultimately, the victims receive transaction messages from their banks for transactions they never made.

Real-Life Example

Mark received an email that looked like it came from a well-known job board, asking him to update his profile information. The email included a link to a fake website that looked almost identical to the real one. When Mark entered his details, cybercriminals captured them.

The Darknet: Information for Sale

Have you seen an iceberg? You can only see 10% or 20% above the surface; the rest, 80% or 90%, is hidden below the water. Let's assume the internet is like an iceberg; from shopping to websites, you can access everything. What we know on the internet is the tip of the iceberg.

But are you aware of what happens on the other part of the internet? Just like the iceberg below the sea hides a larger chunk of ice, the internet contains something called the

"Darknet," which is vast and dangerous. For your knowledge and safety, we will share some secrets about the Darknet in the next section.

What is the Darknet?

Anything illegal or not accessible to the public for privacy or safety reasons on the internet can easily be found on the Darknet. In short, it is the illicit version of the internet, hence the name. From selling your data to purchasing weapons, cybercriminals or criminals engage in all sorts of illegal activities on this platform.

Furthermore, you cannot access these sites through traditional search engines. Such a platform requires technical software like "Tor." Cybercriminals use search engines like "Onion" (an alternate version of Google) to find anything they want.

So, what have you learned since Chapter 1? Yes, the stolen data from your resume might be sold for illegal activities on Darknet. Additionally, cybercriminals may use your information to commit heinous crimes.

Here is how your information is used:

- **Financial Fraud:** After buying your sensitive data from the Darknet, the cybercriminal accesses your bank accounts, may take out loans, or apply for credit cards in your name.
- **Identity Theft:** Scammers create a duplicate profile using your date of birth, full name, and address to perpetrate another scam in your name. Thus, the victim faces long-term problems with their credit and identity.

Real-Life Example

Emily's personal information, including her resume details, was stolen and sold on the Darknet. This information was then used by multiple criminals to open bank accounts and credit lines in her name, causing significant financial and emotional distress.

Social Engineering: Manipulation and Deception

In your childhood, you may have noticed your parents or relatives luring you to sing or dance by offering candies or toys. Social engineering works just like that! Many job seekers do not know how scary this is and how easily a human mind can be manipulated into doing something. Unknowingly, they end up sharing their sensitive data, and the crime chain continues. Later on, your stolen information is used to deceive and manipulate others.

What is Social Engineering?

According to the dictionary, social engineering means psychologically manipulating an individual into doing something unknowingly, such as sharing confidential information. It leaves the person shattered after performing actions they weren't aware of. Social engineering mainly exploits human psychology by playing mental games with the victim. Later, this information is used to fool others by appearing trustworthy and credible.

Here are two examples:

- ➢ A page that offers jobs on a social media platform asks you to open a link to fill in your resume, social media accounts, and passwords. Later, they hack your accounts and steal your personal information.

- You receive a call from a recruiter asking for a telephone interview. They ask for your email IDs, bank details, and other data. In the middle of the call, they ask whether you have received any digits (OTP) through a message. Next, they create a fake yet convincing story to make you share the OTP. Once you share those numbers, they empty your bank accounts in seconds.

Some Common Social Engineering Techniques

- **Pretexting:** It means creating an imaginary scenario or acting like a professional employer to gain access to your personal information. For example, a fake recruiter or HR representative might ask for your address to verify your details.
- **Phishing:** Sending formal emails or text messages while pretending to be a professional company and asking for information.
- **Baiting:** Promising a better opportunity by asking job seekers to perform specific tasks, such as sharing a sample of their work or providing sensitive information.
- **Quid Pro Quo:** Offering benefits, free goodies, or services by exchanging private data, such as sharing your name and contact number to receive free career counseling.

Real-Life Example

A cybercriminal posing as a recruiter contacted Sarah, claiming she had an excellent job opportunity. They requested her social security number and banking details to process her application. Excited about the opportunity, Sarah provided the information, only to realize later that it was a scam designed to steal her identity and money.

Other Risks to Be Aware Of

There are a few more online scams that many job seekers are not aware of, such as:

1. **Data Breaches :** Cybercriminals attempt to access data stored in company databases by hacking the server. They can gain sensitive information. What if you have shared your resume with a company and it was breached?

Real-Life Example

Moster.com, a major job board, experienced a data breach, exposing the personal information of millions of users. This data was later found being sold on the Darknet.

2. **Malware and Ransomware:** A hacker creates malicious software that corrupts, gains, or damages your files in your computer system. Once your data is stolen, the hacker uses it for illegal activities.

Real-Life Example

A job seeker downloaded what they thought was a job application form, only to find it was malware that compromised their computer and stole sensitive information.

3. **Overexposure to Multiple Platforms:** Uploading your resume on every job portal might expose you to threats. Furthermore, any fake job recruiter can access your resume and store the data for future illegal use.

Real-Life Example

Tom posted his resume on several job boards. He later discovered that his information was being used for fraudulent activities without his consent. He was unsure how it happened.

Know these scams and risks to safeguard yourself. Furthermore, if you notice scammers on online job boards, avoid them at all costs. In the next chapter, let's discuss some essential tips to keep your online identity safe.

Chapter-3

Survey Insights

Introduction

We conducted a survey to understand job seekers' perspectives about online privacy and data sharing. This helped us provide more accurate results for the targeted groups. The primary aim of this survey was to understand how job seekers are worried about sharing their personal information online and the missing features they are looking for on online job boards. In the end, we gathered insights and drew conclusions regarding their concerns about data privacy. Let's take a deeper look at this survey to understand it better.

Participants and Demographics

Job seekers from diverse age groups participated in this survey. It helped us to collect data on various demographics, such as:

Age Group

Ages 18-35	20%
Ages 36-45	50%
Ages 46+	30%

Education Level

Undergraduate degrees	60%
Graduate degrees	30%
Other forms of education or professional certifications	10%

Industry of Employment

IT and Technology	Education: 25%
Education	20%
Healthcare and pharmaceuticals	15%
Service Industries	10%
Others	30%

The above demographic tables give us insights into their concerns about personal data being shared on job boards.

Survey Questions and Responses

1. **Familiarity with Identity Theft and `Online Privacy Concerns:** In the first question, on a scale of 1 to 10, the participants were asked to rate how familiar they were with identity theft. The average familiarity score was approximately 5.

   Detailed Insights:

   - **Educational Level:** The participants with graduate degrees were more aware of identity theft and privacy issues, with their average familiarity score being around 7. This shows that the graduates have a great deal of knowledge that can easily be accessed through educational resources.

- **Age Group:** Participants in the younger age groups (18 to 35 years) had lower awareness than the graduates. Their average score was approximately 4. This showcases a need for conducting educational campaigns and programs to raise online safety awareness among younger age groups.
- **Industry:** Individuals in the IT and Technology field showed higher familiarity scores. The average score in this area was around 7. The score was high due to professional exposure to regular updates on data protection topics and cybersecurity.

2. **Personal Experiences with Identity Theft:** One of the survey questions asked the participants if they or someone they knew had ever been a victim of identity theft. Their responses were 45% yes and 55% no.

   Detailed Insights:

   - **Industry Impact:** 60% of people in this field have reported that they have experienced personal and indirect identity thefts, which indicates that these industries are more prone to cyber threats.
   - **Age Factor:** 55% of people aged 46 and above affirmed that they know someone likely to be targeted by identity theft. There could be two possible reasons behind this:
     - More prolonged exposure to online activities.
     - More extensive digital footprints accumulated over time.

- **Preventive Measures:** Survey participants who had experienced identity theft were more likely to use advanced security measures, such as multi-factor authentication and regular credit monitoring.

3. **Safety When Sharing Personal Information Online:** The survey asked participants to rate how safe they feel when sharing their personal information online while job hunting, on a scale from 1 to 10. The average response was 6.

   Detailed Insights:

   - **IT and Technology Professionals:** Participants working in this area felt safer, with an average score of 7, which is excellent. This indicates greater confidence in protecting their personal data due to better knowledge and awareness of cybersecurity.
   - **Education and Service Industries:** Participants in these industries gave the lowest, with an average score of around 5. The survey respondents were worried about receiving fewer resources and less knowledge about how to protect their personal data.
   - **Demographic Variations:** Participants falling into the age bracket of 18 to 35 years reported feeling less safe, with an average score of 5. They feel less secure because of the heavy personal information transfer on social media and online platforms.

4. **Concerns About Posting Resumes on Job Boards:** This area of survey explored participants' concerns about sharing their resumes on job platforms.

Privacy and Security	40%
Spam and Unwanted Contacts	30%
Data Breaches and Hacking Incidents	20%
Others	10%

Detailed Insights:

- **Privacy and Security:** 50% of participants in the 36 to 45 age groups have major concerns about online privacy and security. This age group is always cautious about uploading personal information on online job boards because of past experiences with scammers or more excellent knowledge of privacy issues.
- **Spam and Unwanted Contacts:** People falling under the 18 to 35 age group were more worried about receiving spam messages and emails. Around 35% of these participants expressed concern about this problem. These participants are heavy users of social media and other online platforms, increasing their chances of encountering spammers.
- **Data Breaches:** Around 25% of the healthcare and pharmaceutical field participants are worried about data breaches and hacking incidents. Sensitive information is regularly passed in this field, making it more vulnerable to data threats.

5. **Missing Features or Services in Current Job Search Platforms :** Here are the responses of participants when asked about features or services they feel are missing from current job search platforms:

Reference Hiring	25%
Enhanced Privacy Controls	20%
Comprehensive Spam Filters	15%
Others	40%

Detailed Insights:

- **Reference Hiring:** Around 30% of participants in managerial and professional roles indicated a preference for reference hiring. The main motive is to help verify the job candidates' credentials, gradually enhancing trust in the hiring process.
- **Enhanced Privacy Controls:** 25% of those working in the healthcare and pharmaceutical industries expressed a need for this feature, which can help them protect personal data and give job portal users more control over their information.
- **Comprehensive Spam Filters:** Up to 25% of the participants feel this feature is a need of the hour. Around 20% of people in the education and services sector highlighted this as a missing feature. If job boards install this feature, job seekers can focus on genuine job opportunities and reduce unwanted contacts.

Conclusion

The survey not only helped us find the preferences of job seekers regarding online privacy but also highlighted the loopholes in online job portals. The participants demanded that privacy controls be increased, reference hiring features be added, and privacy controls be enhanced. If all job seekers' needs are met, the online job search portals will become a safe place, improving their job-hunting experience overall.

Chapter-4

Practical Tips For Job Seekers

How to Protect Your Personal Information

Your data privacy is in your hands, so you must stay up-to-date with current data safety happenings. You also need to ensure that your job search is secure. In today's generation, protecting your online identity has become necessary. Besides, every job seeker, regardless of their level, faces issues while looking for a job. So, let's go through some practical steps to address these challenges.

1. **Use Privacy Settings on Job Boards or Job Platforms:** Make sure your personal information is not visible to the public. Plus, ensure that only approved or verified people are allowed to access your resume. By doing so, you reduce the risk of data theft. Otherwise, you can use professional job portals that restrict access to selected employees.

   Moreover, search for jobs on reputed job boards and avoid venturing into new job sites that do not have high-tech privacy features. If you are a new user, ensure your privacy settings are always on. On the other hand, only those job portals that follow international data protection laws should be used.

2. **Create a Separate Email for Job Applications:** Create a professional email address that reflects your career during job search, such as firstname.lastname@examples.com or firstname.careername@example.com. Make sure that the email address is not linked to any bank account. It will help keep you safe from phishing attempts or spam emails while keeping your personal and private life separate.

   If you are concerned about your sensitive data, you can use encrypted email services or an authorized phishing and malware protection tool supported globally.

3. **Avoid Posting Sensitive Information:** Do not add your complete house address; instead, you can write your state and country name. Moreover, avoid mentioning your Social Security Number, birth date, and other sensitive data. Exclude your contact number as well. If you have an official professional website or networking account like LinkedIn, you can add it to your resume and showcase it as a portfolio. Lastly, you can add hobbies, relevant soft skills, hard skills, and technical skills.

4. **Verify Job Postings and Employers:** Do in-depth research about recruiters, employers, the company, and the job posting. Moreover, cross-check the company's founder's name, website, and contact details. Make sure the company and the employer have legitimate and verified profiles on LinkedIn or any other professional networking site with a robust verification process.

Additionally, join professional groups, job forums, and other authentic sites to find out all the details about the potential employer. Additionally, you can directly reach out to the company to ask anything related to the job posting. If you still need clarification and are looking for a job, ask someone from your close circle to help you find the right job.

5. **Use Encrypted Communication Tools:** You can use any safe encrypted communication tool, platform, or service to send emails or other sensitive data safely through email or other communication channels. Alternatively, you can join a secured group to find jobs and share your resumes.

Whether you are a fresher, an experienced professional, or a veteran, don't forget to follow these tips for life. And remember, when it comes to sharing personal information while hunting for a job, "less is more."

Chapter-5

Features of a Secure Job Search Platform

What to Look for in a Safe Job Search Platform

You have all the skills and qualities required for a job role. However, finding a safe job search platform has become tiresome. And today, almost every job board is filled with scammers. Hence, there is a desperate need to be a part of job search platforms that have various security features to protect your personal information.

Fortunately, various job search sites and apps offer safety features. So, let's review these safety elements and how they protect job seekers. For better understanding, we will also share some real-life examples and additional tips to control who can access your sensitive data.

1. Advanced Privacy Controls

Job seekers constantly fear losing their personal information to online scams and unauthorized parties. But rest assured! Various job search platforms now offer numerous options to hide your data, such as personal information visibility, who can see your "About" section, and who can access your documents or other important data. You are the sole owner of your information, and you have total control over your account. If any reputed employer wants to access your files and personal information, you can approve its release.

Real-Life Example

Amanda, a recent graduate, used a job board that allowed her to hide her contact details and only reveal them once she had vetted and approved potential employers. This feature helped her avoid unsolicited contacts and ensured her information was only shared with legitimate employers.

Tips for Job Seekers:

- **Set Your Resume to Private on Job Boards:** You can make your resume private or visible only to you or selected people.
- **Selective Sharing:** Forward your resumes to only relevant and trustworthy companies or employers rather than keeping them visible to the public.
- **Control Visibility:** Check your privacy settings and update your job board apps to see if they have released a newer version of data protection.

2. Robust Verification Processes

Concerns about receiving fake job offers and unsolicited emails are on the rise. Before sharing your personal information, make sure to verify the company, employer, and other details. A legitimate company will always keep its websites and job portals up-to-date with correct information.

Real-Life Example

David, a mid-career professional, used a job platform that verified all employer identities before allowing them to post jobs. This reduced the number of spam and scam job offers he received and increased his confidence in the job search process.

Tips for Job Seekers:

- **Research Employers:** Research potential employers and companies before applying to verify their legitimacy. Look for official websites, LinkedIn profiles, and other authentic portals about the company.
- **Use Verified Platforms:** Stick to job boards and platforms known for their stringent verification processes.
- **Report Suspicious Listings:** If you spot a suspicious job posting on the job board, immediately report it to the platform administrators via email or their site. This makes things easier for other job seekers.

3. Two-Factor Authentication (2FA)

Data breaches can happen to any professional job search platform. Whether you uploaded your resume a few days back or ten years ago, your document is still in their system. Adding an extra layer of protection to shield your sensitive data will keep you away from identity thefts and other cybercrimes.

Real-Life Example

Lisa, a career changer, enabled two-factor authentication on her job search accounts. Even when a breach occurred on a job board she used, her account remained secure because the hackers couldn't bypass the second layer of verification.

Tips for Job Seekers:

- **Enable 2FA:** Turn on two-factor authentication on all job-hunting sites.
- **Use Authentication Apps:** Use trustworthy apps like Google Authenticator or Authy.
- **Regularly Update Passwords:** Make your password strong by adding unique characters such as "@$&*()#."

4. Encrypted Communication

Sometimes, a job seeker who is currently an executive-level employee hunts for a job but is worried about their current employer finding out. Such job candidates need to secure all communications between themselves and the potential employers. This will not only save them from their current employer's scrutiny but also keep their sensitive data safe.

Real-Life Example

John, an executive-level professional, communicated with potential employers through an encrypted messaging job platform. It ensured that his job search remained confidential and that his current employer couldn't intercept any communications.

Tips for Job Seekers:

- **Use Secure Messaging Tools:** Communicate through encrypted messaging or emailing services only.
- **Avoid Public Wi-Fi:** Never use public Wi-Fi while opening job-searching sites. Such networks are highly prone to security breaches.
- **Encrypt Emails:** While using your email address, messaging, or telephonic communication; use only end-to-end encryption.

5. Data Encryption and Storage

Protect your stored personal data from data breaches on job boards. Furthermore, create a backup of your important files and save them to a secured site or app.

Real-Life Example

Sarah, a freelancer, chose a job platform known for its strong data encryption and storage practices. When a breach occurred, her encrypted data remained secure and unreadable to unauthorized parties.

Tips for Job Seekers:

- **Choose Platforms with Strong Encryption:** Use job search boards with advanced encryption services.
- **Regularly Monitor Accounts:** Check your job hunt accounts for any unusual activities.
- **Backup Your Data:** Backup your resume, portfolios, and other job application data on a secured storage site or app.

Additional Features to Look For While Using Job Search Boards

1. **Customizable Privacy Settings**
   - **Know It's Important:** Your privacy needs may vary from those of other job seekers. Make sure to customize the privacy settings according to your needs and situation.
   - **Example**: Anna, an international job seeker, adjusted her privacy settings to comply with local and global data protection laws.
2. **Job Application Tracking**
   - **Know It's Important:** Knowing which employers have accessed your resume can help you manage your job search more effectively.
   - **Example:** Mike, returning to the workforce, used a job board that provided detailed tracking of which employers viewed his resume and when.

3. **User Education and Resources**

   - **Know It's Important:** Stay educated and keep up-to-date on online security. Enroll or register on platforms offering job seekers guides and tips on data safety.
   - **Example:** Tom, a veteran, utilized educational resources provided by his job platform to learn about protecting his personal information during his job search.

These job search platforms are a boon to our kind; however, they have a long way to go. Besides, use platforms that offer 360-degree security, user-friendly security features and customizable settings to protect your resume and other personal data.

Chapter-6

Action Plan for Job Seekers

Your Job Search Security Checklist

Stringent measures should be taken to protect your personal information. In this chapter, we have shared checklists to help you find the right and secure job.

Here's What You Need to Do Before Posting Your Resume Online

1. **Adjust Privacy Settings on Job Boards**
    - **Set Your Resume to Private:** Ensure your resume and other personal details are visible only to verified employers and companies.
    - **Control Information Access:** Do not make your private details visible to the public. Check the privacy updates on the online job portal.

2. **Create a Separate Email Account for Job Applications**
    - **Professional Email Address:** Make a new professional email account for job searching.
    - **Spam and Phishing Protection:** Pick the best email services or providers that offer complete data protection.
3. **Exclude Sensitive Information from Your Resume**
    - **Personal Details:** Exclude your complete address, full name, Social Security Number, and date of birth.
    - **General Location:** Add only your state and country instead of your complete address.
4. **Verify the Legitimacy of Job Postings and Employers**
    - **Research Companies:** Check the company and employer information on LinkedIn or other websites.
    - **Contact Employers Directly:** If you have any questions related to the job role, you can contact the company's HR for clarification.
    - **Use Verified Platforms:** Choose only those job boards or websites with verified employers.
5. **Use Secure Communication Tools**
    - **Encrypted Email Services:** Go for secure communication services like ProtonMail while sharing personal details.
    - **Secure Messaging Apps:** Use secured texting and calling tools like WhatsApp or Signal.

6. **Use My Safe Resume like products**
    - **My Safe Resume**: A product like My Safe Resume can help you safeguard your personal information or any other details you choose to include on your resume.

During Your Job Search

7. **Monitor Your Online Presence**
    - **Google Yourself:** Check your name regularly on the Internet. This will help you understand how your name appears on Google.
    - **Social Media Privacy:** Keep your social media accounts private by adding only known potential employers and limiting the visibility of your personal data.
8. **Be Wary of Phishing Scams**
    - **Check Email Addresses:** Verify the authenticity of employers' and companies' email addresses. Also, see if their emails are from legitimate company domains.
    - **Avoid Clicking Unknown Links:** Never click on unknown links from suspicious employers or sources.
9. **Use Strong, Unique Passwords**
    - **Password Managers:** Generate and store strong passwords using password managers like 1Password or LastPass.
    - **Regular Updates:** Change your passwords frequently and never use the same passwords for different job portal IDs.
10. **Track Your Applications**
    - **Application Records:** Keep a record of all the jobs you apply for daily, including the employer name, job role,

company name, and company details like My Safe Resume offers you a job tracker.

- **Follow-Up:** After an interview or resume submission, follow up to know the current status.

11. **Be Mindful of Job Offer Red Flags**

- **Upfront Payments:** It's a red flag if a company or the employer asks for application or training fees.
- **Too Good to Be True:** If the job role and the salary package seem beyond your imagination, then the job is probably fake.

Once You Get a New Job

12. **Remove Your Resume from Job Boards**

- **Deactivate Accounts:** After posting your resume on specific job boards, delete or deactivate your accounts.
- **Remove Personal Information:** Remove all your data, such as your resume, portfolios, and other job-related materials, from the public view.

13. **Update Your Online Profiles**

- **LinkedIn:** Add new details, like your new job profile, for your connections to see.
- **Other Platforms:** Update your new job role to other professional networking sites.
- **My Safe Resume:** Keep your My Safe Resume subscription active to stay informed about who is attempting to access your information.

14. **Secure Your New Job Information**
    - **Company Policies:** Familiarize yourself with the company's and your employer's data security policies.
    - **Protect Company Data:** Do not share the company's sensitive information or details about current or upcoming projects with anyone, offline or online.
15. **Change Passwords and Security Questions**
    - **Update Security:** To keep your email address secure from theft, frequently change your passwords and security questions.
16. **Notify Your Network**
    - **Professional Contacts:** If you want to notify your other professional networks about your new job role, do so discreetly and without sharing any personal data.
    - **Social Media Announcement:** You can publicly announce your new position on LinkedIn or other social media accounts without oversharing.

Additional Tips for Ongoing Security

1. **Regularly Review Privacy Settings**
    - **Routine Checks:** Do not forget to review and update your privacy settings on all job portals and professional and social networking sites.
    - **Stay Informed:** Keep yourself updated about the latest privacy policies and settings on all your professional and social networking sites.
2. **Use Virtual Private Networks (VPNs)**
    - **Secure Connections:** Always use a VPN when using public Wi-Fi while searching for jobs.

3. **Keep Your Devices Secure**
    - **Antivirus Software:** Research, install, and regularly update anti-malware or antivirus software.
    - **Secure Backups:** Regular data backups on safe storage apps or services can protect your personal data for a long time.
4. **Educate Yourself on Cybersecurity**
    - **Stay Updated:** Stay informed about the latest online threats and ways to protect your data against them.
    - **Take Courses:** Join forums or enroll in online or offline courses to learn about cybersecurity and how to secure your data in the online world.
5. **Seek Professional Help if Needed**
    - **Consult Experts:** If you face any issues when searching for jobs on online portals, seek guidance from cybersecurity professionals.

If you have reached this far, then you must have understood how to safeguard your resume and other job-related data while reducing the risks of online job search fraud. Additionally, once you get your dream job, remove all personal data from the job search portals.

Chapter-7

Additional Resources

Tools and Resources for Job Seekers

In addition to the strategies and tips, various tools and resources can help you safeguard your personal information and navigate the job market securely. Here are some of the most effective resources you can utilise:

1. Password Managers

Tools like LastPass or 1Password can be used to store and generate strong passwords.

Why It's Important

Using a password manager helps you create and manage complex, unique passwords for all your accounts, reducing the risk of breaches due to weak or reused passwords.

Recommended Tools:

- **LastPass:** Stores encrypted passwords online and autofills login details for websites.
- **1Password:** Offers secure password storage, password generation, and integrated two-factor authentication (2FA).

2. Two-Factor Authentication Apps

Consider using Google Authenticator or Authy for added security.

Why It's Important

Two-factor authentication adds an extra layer of security by requiring a second verification form, such as a code sent to your phone in addition to your password.

Recommended Tools:

- **Google Authenticator:** Generates 2FA codes on your phone for added security.
- **Authy:** Provides multi-device support and backup options for 2FA.

3. Identity Theft Protection Services

Services like LifeLock or IdentityGuard are used to monitor and protect your identity.

Why It's Important

These services monitor your personal information for signs of identity theft and assist you if your identity is compromised.

Recommended Services:

- **LifeLock:** Offers comprehensive identity theft protection, including credit monitoring and alerts.
- **IdentityGuard:** Provides continuous monitoring of your personal information and alerts you to potential threats.

4. Secure Email Providers

Use email services with strong security features to protect your communications.

> **Why It's Important**
>
> Secure email providers offer encryption and advanced security measures to keep your communications private.

Recommended Providers:

- **ProtonMail:** An end-to-end encrypted email service designed to protect user privacy.
- **Tutanota:** Provides encrypted email services with a focus on security and privacy.

5. Virtual Private Networks (VPNs)

Use VPNs to protect your online activity and data.

> **Why It's Important**
>
> VPNs encrypt your internet connection, protecting your data from being intercepted by unauthorised parties, especially on public Wi-Fi.

Recommended VPNs:

- **NordVPN:** Offers robust encryption and a strict no-logs policy.
- **ExpressVPN:** Known for high-speed connections and robust security features.

6. Antivirus and Anti-Malware Software

Protect your devices from malicious software.

Why It's Important

Antivirus and anti-malware software detect and remove threats that could compromise your personal information.

Recommended Software:

- **Malwarebytes:** Provides comprehensive protection against malware, ransomware, and other threats.
- **Bitdefender:** Offers real-time protection against viruses, malware, and other cyber threats.

7. Encrypted Cloud Storage

Store your sensitive documents securely in the cloud.

Why It's Important

Encrypted cloud storage protects your files from unauthorised access.

Recommended Services:

- **Sync.com:** Provides end-to-end encrypted cloud storage and file sharing.
- **Tresorit:** Offers secure cloud storage with zero-knowledge encryption.

8. Job Search Platforms with Strong Security Features

Choose job boards and platforms that prioritise user security.

Why It's Important

Secure job search platforms implement measures to protect your personal information from breaches and unauthorised access.

Recommended Platforms:

- **LinkedIn:** Offers privacy controls and encrypted communications.
- **Indeed:** Known for robust verification processes for job postings and employers.
- **Glassdoor:** Provides features to control the visibility of your personal information.

9. Educational Resources on Cybersecurity

Stay informed about the latest cybersecurity threats and protection strategies.

Why It's Important

Knowledge is power. Understanding cybersecurity threats helps you take proactive steps to protect your information.

Recommended Resources:

- **Cybersecurity and Infrastructure Security Agency (CISA):** Offers resources and tips on protecting your online identity.
- **StaySafeOnline.org:** Provides information on the latest cyber threats and how to defend against them.
- **Coursera and Udemy:** Courses on cybersecurity fundamentals and advanced protection techniques are offered.

10. Personal Information Monitoring Tools

Use tools that monitor your personal information for potential security breaches.

Why It's Important

These tools alert you to unauthorised use of your personal information, allowing you to take action quickly.

Recommended Tools:

- **Have I Been Pwned:** Checks if your email or phone number has been patrt of a data breach.
- **PrivacyDuck:** Helps you remove your personal information from data broker websites.

Using these tools and resources, you can significantly enhance your security and protect your personal information throughout your job search. Staying proactive and informed is key to navigating the digital job market safely.

Chapter-8

Conclusion

While Looking For A Job, Stay Safe, Stay Secure!

Your job search should be a step forward in your career, not a risk to your personal information. By following the tips and using the resources in this guide, you can protect your data and focus on finding your next great opportunity.

A Note About MySafeResume.com

At MySafeResume.com, we understand the importance of protecting your personal information during your job search. That's why we've designed a platform with your security in mind, offering features that address the most pressing concerns of job seekers today. In this final section, we'll recap the key Phase 1 features of MySafeResume.com that can help you maintain your privacy and security while job hunting.

Phase 1 Features of MySafeResume.com:

1. **Advanced Privacy Controls:**
   - **Hide Personal Information:** Our platform allows you to hide your personal information, such as your phone number and email address, until you approve its release.
   - **QR Code Integration:** Personal details are stored behind a QR code. Employers can scan the code to request access, ensuring your information is only shared with verified parties.
2. **Email Forwarding:**
   - **Anonymous Communication:** Create an email forwarder through MySafeResume.com to use on job platforms. This ensures your real email address remains private, reducing the risk of spam and phishing attempts.
3. **Multiple Resume Templates:**
   - **Professional Designs:** Choose from various professional resume templates to create multiple versions of your resume tailored to different job applications.
   - **Annual Downloads:** Your subscription allows you to download up to 12 resumes annually. If you need more, you can purchase additional downloads for a nominal fee.
4. **Robust Verification Processes:**
   - **Employer Validation:** Employers and job hunters who wish to access your personal information must validate their email through a one-time password

(OTP) sent to their email. This adds an extra layer of security, ensuring only legitimate entities can view your details.

5. **Notification and Approval System:**
   - **Real-Time Alerts:** Receive notifications when someone requests access to your personal information. You will be informed of the requester's verified email domain (e.g., emailxxxx@company.com).
   - **Control Over Information Sharing:** Approve or deny requests to view your contact details based on the requester's verification. This empowers you to control who gets access to your personal information.
6. **Activity Dashboard:**
   - **Track Requests:** View a history of who has requested your contact details per resume, along with your approval or denial choices.
   - **Prevent Repeated Requests:** Our system prevents repeated requests from the same email, reducing the risk of harassment or unauthorised access attempts.

In Summary

By integrating these features, MySafeResume.com offers a secure and user-friendly platform to support your job search. Our goal is to empower you with the tools and knowledge to safeguard your personal information while you pursue new career opportunities.

Remember, your job search should be a step toward a brighter future, not a source of concern about privacy and security. Stay vigilant, utilize the resources and tips provided in this guide, and take full advantage of the robust features offered by MySafeResume.com.

or if you have any queries, concerns, or simply want to reach out for a conversation, feel free to contact us at

Sachin Diwakar (Author)

https://www.linkedin.com/in/sachindiwaker

Neha Boricha (Co-Author)

https://www.linkedin.com/in/neha-b-23b6a713b

Stay safe, stay secure, and best of luck in your job search!

For more information and to start securing your resume today, visit MySafeResume.com.